**Your Digital Personality**

We all have one.

It is the pool of digital information available to anyone with the right access, tools and motivation to find it.

In our digitised world, it represents your personality.

Increasingly it is the first impression that you make upon others and first impressions are important.

# Your Digital Personality

## A book about

Who owns information about us

What they do with it

What we can do to manage it

## Adam Blackie

ISBN 978-1-4475-9331-7

Published by LuLu.com

This is the first edition. If you would like to suggest improvements for a future edition, please email or visit our website.

suggestions@websmartgroup.co.uk

www.WebSmartGroup.co.uk

This is my first book, dedicated to my family.

Christine, Tom and Harriet.

*With thee every joy enhanced,*

*With thee, delight is ever new,*

*With thee is life incessant bliss,*

*Thine, thine it all shall be.*

- The Creation, Franz Joseph Haydn.

*"I am what is mine. Personality is the original personal property."*

Norman O. Brown


*"Today knowledge has power. It controls access to opportunity and advancement."*

Peter Drucker


*"Privacy is a transient notion. It started when people stopped believing that God could see everything and stopped when governments realised there was a vacancy to be filled."*

Roger Needham


*"You have zero privacy anyway. Get over it."*

Scott McNealy

# Acknowledgements

My thanks go to the staff at the National Archives in Kew, UK, for giving me an understanding of how our personal information is used as a valuable corporate information asset.

Tom Ilube helped me to understand how corporations use, trade and recycle personal financial information.

Pete Cridland, Monu Ogbe for inspiring me to think about writing this book and encouraging me to get on with it.

Tom, Harriet, Moira and Christine for ideas and editing first drafts.

Rob Oldham for final editing.

# Authors Preface

WebSmart is an information consulting and change management business that leads organisations through their change programmes. We work with UK businesses to improve the way their staff and customers use information and technology.

We have noticed that the barriers to using new technology are largely emotional.

Negative emotions often stand in the way of accepting technology change and these emotions obstruct our ability to learn to do things differently.

The predominant negative emotion is fear, of change and of the unknown. This stops us from acting logically.

We need to act logically and learn to manage our own digital information or we may lose the opportunity to do so. Unhappily, this is because other people will create a Digital Personality for us.

We cannot stop this from happening.

Ignoring this trend is not an option.

This book shows you how to take action to protect and manage your Digital Personality.

# Contents

**Information is an asset**

**Assets are valuable**

**Your personal information is an asset**

**Who can you trust to manage your personal information?**

# What is a Digital Personality?

### Do we need a Digital Personality?

Digital Personality is a phrase that describes the idea of an online personal electronic identity. In other words, it could be the "electronic individual" or "digital self".

It is you, but as others see you when they find the personal digital information you leave behind. This is combined with the information that others create about you. This pool of information is semi-permanent and growing and the tools to find and filter it are becoming increasingly sophisticated and easy to use.

Digital Personality is becoming more important to us all because it is now very likely to be the first impression that others have of us.

In a pre-digital world, we were introduced to others via a mutual contact or via a formal invitation. The all-important first impression was created in the first five or ten seconds when we met face to face. The people we met instantly assessed our looks, dress, bearing, handshake and overall image.

First impressions count, they stay with us for a long time.

In a digital world first impressions are delivered online, without our knowledge, to people we do not know and may never meet. Many of us will routinely "Google" a new contact, colleague or boss before we meet them to find out more about them. We may also research our new contacts online soon after we first meet to confirm our initial impressions.

This use of the internet to investigate each other is now possible because the availability and breadth of online information about all of us is increasing every day. Online personal data is gradually changing the way we meet and interact with each other.

Our Digital Personalities are beginning to make an impression upon the social and business networks that we develop.

Having an appropriate profile is becoming increasingly important in all sorts of new relationships.

**Why write this book?**

There is a need to recognise the emergence of Digital Personality, to explore why this might be important to us and to encourage more of us to manage it appropriately.

There is an also imbalance of power between creators of personal information (us) and the users and owners of that information (organisations). As more personal information becomes available, the wider that imbalance is becoming.

People are not yet responding to this fundamental change in the way we assess new contacts. During years of information management consulting with numerous organisations, including working with digital archives and corporate information assets, I noted the range and scope of personal information held by government and non-government archives. I also became aware of the degree to which these organisations rely upon personal information for their day-to-day business.

This experience led to some research with colleagues to understand the emotional and practical impact upon the individuals whose personal information was being stored.

The prevalent emotion amongst us turned out to be fear. We are worried about our privacy. However, there is a conflicting desire. We want to discover more about others, we research them, particularly before we conduct any transaction with them.

It turns out that there is a simple emotional conflict. We want to protect our privacy, but we also want to know more about others, thereby reducing their privacy.

Personal privacy is not the subject of this book. Numerous authors have already written extensively on that subject. I can contribute to their work only by emphasising the ways in which individuals are choosing to sacrifice their personal privacy in order to increase their effectiveness in the digital world.

The ideas in this book describe a move away from the desire for personal privacy towards an emerging need to manage our online image and the risks associated with being visible. In short, to have a Digital Personality we need to publish information about ourselves. In doing this we sacrifice our privacy for a greater benefit. We need to be able to manage our identity to minimise the risks involved with this approach.

In a digital world we must have an online presence in order to communicate and do business with each other. For some organisations, online is now the only way to transact business.[1]   This adds to the accumulated digital and electronic presence that I call the Digital Personality. It is the identity that we use to interact with others.  It is, in effect, our digital self.

To some extent, we can control how we choose to portray ourselves online.  Some of us may already have a separate online identity to our offline one. The creation of this other identity is a common practice amongst bloggers who generally use a pseudonym to protect their real identity.  However, we do not always want to disguise our real identity online; in some encounters we need to be our real selves in order to get to know and trust others.

In many online transactions your Digital Personality already delivers the first impressions of who you are. For the people who encounter you online it is all they have until they meet you in person and in this virtual world they may never actually do that.

This perception of our Digital Personality can be positive, neutral or negative depending upon the recipient's attitudes, viewpoint, beliefs, mores etc. Perceptions of our Digital Personality are based upon

---

[1] E.g. In the UK, from 2010, HM Revenue and Customs will only allow online versions of Value Added Tax returns

similarly subjective criteria to those we use when we first meet in person. They are based upon arbitrary and complex individual and group standards. It is important that we are aware of our Digital Personality, and therefore the personal information available to other people. The key question is "Does your Digital Personality present you in a way that you feel is positive and true to you?"

We all need a Digital Personality. This is because others require it of us, they will be reluctant or unable to transact with us without one. In future, I believe that not having an adequately detailed Digital Personality will eventually be worse than having a negative one. In a world where most transactions and many social interactions will be digital, presenting a blank canvas to others will lead to automatic rejection. Our human need to know more about the people we meet will prompt potential new contacts to seek out alternatives to you. "Better the devil we know than the devil we don't".

We will want to share our Digital Personality with some, we will want to withhold it from others, and we will want our Digital Personality to be a true first impression of us as an individual.

In the meantime, there are clear signs that we are already loosing control over our Digital Personalities. Information about us is constantly created and stored without our direct input or permission. Most of us are only just beginning to realise this and if we allow it to continue, we will loose control over how the world perceives us.

**Who can see our Digital Personality?**

The initial perception of our Digital Personality is governed by the amount of information that is available to a user browsing the web or to a business analysing its databases.  In later chapters of this book we will see that:

- Some information about us is easily available.
- Much more information about us is available to those who have acquired appropriate tools to find it.
- Even more information is available to those who take the trouble to dig for it or know where to find it.

New businesses are emerging to help us and others find information in what has become known as the "deep web".[2]  The deep web is the un-indexed information available on the Internet and because of this, a typical search engine such as Google or Yahoo! will not find it.  This can be for a variety of reasons:

- The businesses that supply search engines have not yet discovered the information.

- The information has been found and has been discounted as unimportant.

- Efficient technologies have not yet been developed for extracting information from obscure datasets. Search engines may not find information if it is buried in, say, a spreadsheet or as an entry in a large database.

- Some web pages contain code that tells search engines to ignore their content, a sort of opt-out clause for web sites.

- Information about you may be contained in archived versions of web sites[3].  By default, search engines do not usually present results from archived sources.

- Web filters often exclude web pages with inappropriate content such as pornography, race hate, violence, etc.

- Searches usually have a preference for a particular language or URL country suffix.

---

[2] Try an online search for "Reputation Defender" to see a selection of tools available for analysing online reputation.
[3] For example see the Internet Archive WayBack Machine – several billions of archived web pages. - http://www.archive.org/web/web.php

In short, regular search engines generally present only part of the information that is available about your Digital Personality.  If you search using appropriate technologies and a wider scope of sources, much more of your Digital Personality can be found, but how many of you would go to these lengths to discover all the information?

In any case, even if you can successfully find and attempt to control your own Digital Personality, you then have the issue of linked Digital Personalities to consider.

**The effects of linking to others**

Linking data from different sources can build a different picture of our Digital Personality. When we start to search for all the information that is available about a Digital Personality, we can widen a search to include all the other Digital Personalities that may be linked with it.

This is known as Social Graphing, and much academic and practical work is already available on this subject, some of which is reviewed in this book.[4] In the real

---

[4] For an example of the academic work in this area see the FIDIS organisation (Future of Identity in an Information Society) a part of the EU funded NoE (Network of Excellence)

world if we really want to know what an individual is like, it is best to ask that person's colleagues, friends, kith and kin and so on. The social group to which we belong and what others say about us is important.

An example of the use of Social Graphing is government employee security vetting. This technique has been used in government to clear employees to use sensitive information.[5] The technique is a paper based process that looks at any available records for an individual and then goes on to interview significant people in that persons life. The theory and practical experience of these techniques concludes that what we say about ourselves is much less important than what others say about us.

The online application of this technique is already used by a number of existing businesses that rely upon reputation reporting as part of their online service. eBay, Amazon and LinkedIn are all examples of businesses that allow members to rate each other's reputation.

eBay and Amazon are online marketplaces and retailers. They ask customers to rate their experience

---

[5]See:http://www.pcg.org.uk/cms/documents/POLICY_AND_CAMPAIGNS/regulation/security clearances/HMG Personnel Security Controls.pdf

for each purchase. The accumulated rating creates a reassurance or warning for new customers for each supplier. A good rating equals a good service and a poor one indicates a supplier to avoid.

LinkedIn is a membership based networking organisation. It asks its members to recommend each other's services. This might be seen as a mutual backslapping exercise, until we understand that the recommendations cannot be retracted. If you recommend a colleague, and they subsequently provide poor service to a third party it will reflect badly on you.

Organisations do this in order that we can evaluate each other's reputation based upon the ratings of others. We may not know them personally, but we have an opinion about the service they have provided.

A good reputation encourages others to transact with us. What other people say about us on these websites really does matter.

For Social Graphing to work well, it needs access to as much information about us as possible, in both a direct and indirect form.

Already there are businesses that will provide a summary of your Social Graphing information for a small fee.[6] This service is a digital extension of a long established offline practice, traditionally only available to the rich and famous, to employ public relations teams to detect, manipulate and manage our reputation and image.

As technology makes the collation, analysis and storage of information increasingly efficient, the cost of creating Social Graphs is falling. In this more efficient world, many digital reputation management businesses are emerging.

If I can find out about you and who is linked to you, then I can build a more comprehensive and useful profile of you as an individual. What this profile means to me and how I act upon it is entirely at my discretion.

Here are some questions that you could ask about Social Graphing and reputation management in general:

- How do we feel about organisations owning and using information about us?
- How will it affect us?
- Will future employers be conducting routine Social Graphs for prospective employees?

---

[6] Start at Pipl.com, or try a general search for people finding services.

- Will employees be subject to annual audits of their Social Graph and be rated accordingly?

- Will future life partners commission a comprehensive Social Graph before finally committing to a relationship?

- How can we use these techniques to make sense of the overwhelming amount of information that is available about other people?

**Our reaction to Digital Personality**

Our psychological reactions to Social Graphing are polarised between our need to remain private and our need to know more about others. We have a tendency to want to divulge less than we collect. The fears that we feel when sharing our information include:

- The potential for our identity to be stolen and used the fraudulent purposes i.e. identity theft.

- The ability of others to impersonate us in an electronic financial system, i.e. in fraudulent use for financial gain.

- Long forgotten events in our life may be resurrected and could embarrass us in later life stages.

- Privacy concerns where business or government has centralised personal information for future and un-specified use.

## Possible management strategies

If we accept the advantages of a Digital Personality to enable transactions with others, what strategies will we need to cope with the fears and possible threats that Social Graphing might cause?

- We could withdraw from the electronic world. This would work if you want to be a modern-day hermit, however if you want to play an active part in society you really do need to be online. In any case, we should not ignore what others may be publishing about us.

- We could start to delete the available information about us in order to prune the depth of information available to others. However, we do not own some information, others own it, and so we may not have the right to delete it.

- We could manage our own Social Profile by using some of the emerging management tools and making regular efforts to keep an eye upon what is being said about us, and on those who are linked to us.

In order to influence the amount of information held about us and used by others, we will need some form of control over it.

## Information ownership

The final chapters of this book address personal information ownership.

In the paper world, the creation of information about individuals was a time-consuming process. Information was difficult to transmit, and therefore was rarely leaked or mislaid in bulk. Therefore, the cost of its accumulation and the relatively low risk of paper records being disseminated were good enough reasons for the data to remain in the ownership of those who created it.

In the information management age, creating a database of information about individuals can be as easy as trawling the Internet for all the available information that has been created by the individuals and their contacts, or by simply acquiring a data set from another organisation. Gathering, analysis, storage and archiving of information is far cheaper and easier than it has ever been. It seems that the transfer of ownership from the originator (us) to the user (an organisation) has been taken for granted.

In the paper world, the cost of keeping information was high. Paper archives need space, maintenance teams and they incur costs each time an item is retrieved. In the paper world, most information is scrapped because of the costs and practicalities of keeping it.

In the digital world reductions in the cost of storage and retrieval have changed the dynamics of decisions to keep data. The manual effort of sorting, filtering and deleting information from data sets is now much more expensive than keeping everything. Therefore, the default decision of most organisations tends to be at the dataset level. If a data set has any sort of current or future value, the default decision will often be to keep it all. The obvious risk here is that some of the information leaks into the public domain. Once it is there, it is very difficult to remove.

Unlike paper based information, it is easy to leak or lose digital information and as many organisations have experienced in the recent past, much more likely. A succession of data losses in the nineties and noughties has in turn led to a recent emphasis upon information security. A recent example of this is the leaking of large amounts of American based inter-government communications to an organisation campaigning for freedom of information. The organisation is called WikiLeaks[7]. They have encouraged the concept of whistle-blowing to good effect. They have made themselves into an

---

[7] Current URL - http://213.251.145.96/, but this changes frequently, so it is best to just search for the name WikiLeaks.

international brand in a very short period and have demonstrated a surprising degree of robustness by surviving concerted attempts by the authorities to close them down. Is this the start of an emerging industry based upon the inability of large organisations to keep their data safe?

The concept of information security or keeping information safe for an organisation has reinforced the concept of organisational ownership and stewardship. It is therefore unlikely that an organisation that holds information about an individual will readily accept that the individual should have any say in the use and continued existence of that information. They will be reluctant to surrender ownership of something that they are trying so hard to protect.

## Who owns your Digital Personality?

This book concludes by considering whether a paradigm shift in the concepts of personal information ownership may be required at some point in the future.  If Social Graphing becomes the norm, and individuals continue to have few proactive management rights over the information held about them, we will inexorably lose control over our Digital Personality.

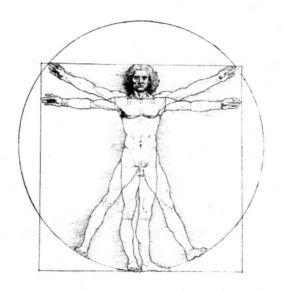

**How important are perfect proportions?**

# Social Graphing and Profiling

### Knowing about others

Who we are is important to us and to other people. We like to know with whom we are dealing. It makes us feel safe.

In the pre-digital world, life may have been simpler. Relationships developed with others over a longer period; they were expected to last a long time. New contacts were often introduced via a mutual acquaintance that both parties knew and trusted. This process meant we could largely rely upon others to alert us to unreliable or suspicious individuals.

In the digital world, we are introduced to new contacts on a daily basis. Email, online shopping, remote contact centres, wiki collaboration, blog comments and friend suggestions on FaceBook are some of the places where we meet new people. The formal introduction is an increasingly rare event.

So how certain are we that the new digital contacts that we meet are whom they say they are?

There are several steps that we can take to establish their credentials, including:

- We can Google their name or email address and see what comes up (this often produces a lot of random and unrelated information).

- We can check out the popular social and business networking sites such as FaceBook or LinkedIn and see what they say about themselves (this gives us their own version of their story).

- We can check out the links and recommendations that they have to others on their social networking sites to get a sense of what their personal networks look like (this is time consuming).

- We can employ a third party to do a Social Graph analysis for us (this will have a cost).

These steps represent an increasingly complex set of search and analysis techniques each following on logically from the other.

The number of steps that we take along this path is dependent upon just two factors. First, how important is it for us to be certain who the other person is, and second, is the information worth the time and money to find it?

This generates interesting and simple formula as follows:

How much we are willing to dig $= f$ {time x money}

We know that technology has already, and will continue to, reduce the costs on the right hand side of the equation. As these reduce, people will be more willing to pay for a Social Graph analysis.

Developments in this field are driven by a variety of inter-related factors:

- The increasing power of database technologies used for social and business networking, population surveillance, personal communication, performance measurement and process tracking, long term data storage, and information transfer.

- The use of information in more complex organisational decision-making. Automation of the initial stages of decision-making develops methods to track our choices and preferences for future analysis.

- A gradual improvement in links between corporate datasets plus the ability to purchase and combine third party datasets is creating a more detailed picture of individuals. These aggregations can include intimate details about a person and their activities.

Technology has provided the tools and corporate information management techniques that have indirectly led to the development of individual Social Graphing.

## What is Social Graphing?

It is early days. Techniques are developing, mostly led by communication professionals, marketing analysts and academics.

The definition of Social Graphing in this context is:

---

**Social Graphing**

The collection of available personal information that is collated for use in an automated process that is designed to categorise people into types, groups, common units, etc

---

**Figure 1 - Defining Social Graphing**

Social Graphing has been indirectly developed by social networking, marketing and sales professionals to identify groups of individuals as part of a larger target group. These target groups are a market for their product or service. It has been described as "the global mapping of everybody and how they're related".[8]

Their process generally uses some form of scoring or ranking mechanism to place individuals into a relevant category. These categories are accurate enough to

---

[8] http://www.cbsnews.com/stories/2010/04/21/tech/main6418458.shtml

launch a marketing campaign and this is usually where the analysis ends.

However, this is the point at which I became interested, because there is a by-product of interesting personal data that is ignored by the generic profiling approach.

As we have seen, the demand for generic market profiling has led to the development of techniques for data filtering and analysis, so now the data for individuals is relatively easy to isolate from the data sets.[9]

The range of indicators that are available for analysis is only limited by the search terms that we use, and the ones that we use are only limited by our imagination.

Readily available tools can then assist us in the search for meaning in the data. Once we have identified the data, many search engines allow us to export that data into other, more user friendly, computer programs for further sifting and analysis. This means that a person with reasonable skills in Microsoft Excel

---

[9] Here we are talking about search algorithms that can look for multiple search terms and automatically identify other terms that might be similar. E.g., the way in which Google guesses that you have misspelled a word.

or Access[10] can quickly sort a long list of possible results into a much shorter list of probable ones.

From here, the techniques of Individual Social Graphing are used and human effort and application of intelligence takes over.

Privacy erosion seems to be creeping up slowly. The gradual improvement in linkages between datasets is creating a more detailed picture of individuals. These aggregations of information can include intimate details about a person and their activities. The inexpensive and easy to use data analysis tools for manipulating the data are available to anyone, and the only limit to their use is the imagination and talent of the analyst.

Social Graphing uses the concept of synergy. i.e. the whole is more than the sum of its parts; it makes the development of new information relationships possible. These information relationships are formed without the subjects' permission or knowledge. We may have contributed information about ourselves freely to a number of separate databases but it is unlikely that we will have anticipated the effect of

---

[10] Excel and Access are market leading data storage and analysis tools. They are available at very low cost.

merging the data, especially where that merger might reveal something more about us.

Put simply, when we have more connections we can build a more complex and comprehensive picture.

The diagram below illustrates that when increasing numbers of datasets are linked together the complexity of the links is rapidly multiplied. As the links increase, the value of the information being analysed becomes much more than the sum of its parts. Note that when 10 datasets are linked there will be 45 connections, with 15 datasets there will be 105 and so on.

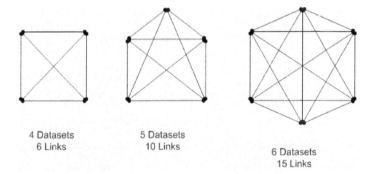

4 Datasets
6 Links

5 Datasets
10 Links

6 Datasets
15 Links

**Figure 2 - How Networks Become Exponential**

The synergy we achieve when we merge datasets is something that most of us do not fully appreciate. Each additional piece of information reveals more and more about us. This is the hidden process providing the real power behind Social Graphing.

## Linking our Digital Personality to others

The impact of linking our Digital Personality to other people in our network adds another level of complexity to the Social Graph that is available.

If the person represented in the centre of the diagram below is presenting themselves as "Type 1" and we can see that their linked Digital Personality profiles are mostly "Type 2" does this give us a cause for concern? The answer is possibly yes, but only where the differences between the types are so wide that there is a clear cause for concern. E.g., where Type 1 is Financial Manager and Type 2 is Fraudster.

The degree of difference that is acceptable in this type of Social Graphing analysis is unique in every case. Moreover, it will be individual analysts who will be making these decisions, and the decisions will be based upon crude alerts from an automated system. This is the existing approach that many credit businesses take when deciding upon a new loan application. Their systems process, and then automatically approve the cases where the credit scoring is sufficient. Any discrepancies from these norms are then referred to an agent for manual review. The agents take the final decision about whether to lend or not. A key indicator in the decision is the presence of conflicting information.

When social graphing becomes part of our normal business decision-making processes, we will need to rely upon human judgement to "approve" any doubtful graphs. Agents, who can only make the best of the information presented to them, will assess those of us who do not pass through any automated stages.

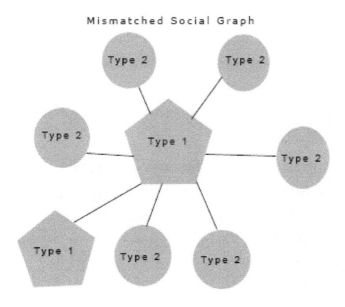

**Figure 3 - Mismatched Social Graph**

## Why this is an issue?

So do we need to worry? The answer to this is that it depends upon how the Social Graphing technique is used. It can be put to positive use e.g. to identify criminals and their networks of activities and to less positive use e.g. to provide political knowledge for use against a rival.

Here are some examples of how Social Graphing and Profiling information could influence your life. These are in both professional and personal contexts, to show that these techniques really can affect any part of our lives.

They are included here to demonstrate that these techniques are currently being used in a narrow, website specific context. It is a relatively small step from here to generic techniques applied to us all.

The first example is taken from a 2010 web page and an email communication from LinkedIn,[11] a major social networking site. One LinkedIn quote points to a collaborative system where people help each other, the next to a more judgemental (or exclusive) approach to using information about us.

---

[11] www.LinkedIn.com

---

**From the LinkedIn "about us" page**

**Relationships Matter**
Your professional network of trusted contacts gives you an advantage in your career, and is one of your most valuable assets. LinkedIn exists to help you make better use of your professional network and help the people you trust in return. Our mission is to connect the world's professionals to make them more productive and successful. We believe that in a global connected economy, your success as a professional and your competitiveness as a company depends upon faster access to insight and resources you can trust.

**....and from a 2010 email I received from LinkedIn.**

DID YOU KNOW **you can conduct a more credible and powerful reference check using LinkedIn?**
Enter the company name and years of employment or the prospective employee to find their colleagues that are also in your network. This provides you with a more balanced set of feedback to evaluate that new hire.

---

**Figure 4 - LinkedIn on Reference Checking**

The second example is from the eHarmony[12] dating website. It tells us how they use Social Graphing techniques to match customers with a potentially compatible partner. One quote extols the virtues of profiling techniques as a successful way to match us to a potential life partner; and the next quote points us to the dangers of having a profile containing anything that may be perceived as negative. Negative comments undermine our Digital Personality.

---

[12] www.eHarmony.co.uk

---

**From the eHarmony "why it works" page.**

**eHarmony UK** is different
eHarmony is more than just another online dating site. The eHarmony Compatibility Matching System™ measures your compatibility with our singles to match you with men/women with whom you share deep levels of compatibility. Where other sites make you search through pictures and paragraphs, eHarmony matches you based on your compatibility in the most important areas of life – such as character, intellect, sense of humour, spirituality, values, beliefs, passion, and other key dimensions.

**....and eHarmony's advice on profiling.**

**The profile**
More bad news, we can't tell you what to write that will portray who you honestly are. .,......... What we can do however, is tell you what not to write. Scientifically speaking, there are some things – listed below – that you can exclude, for profile success.

Source:http://www.eharmony.co.uk/relationship-advice/using-eharmony/2010/01/what-not-to-say-in-your-about-me-profile

---

**Figure 5 - eHarmony on Profiling**

Finally, a simple example of a Social Profiling technique applied by insurance companies to determine how big our pension payments might be.

Pensions benefits can be determined by where we live. This example comes from a news story sent by the financial services provider Lansdown Hargreaves[13] to their customers in November 2010.

---

[13] www.h-l.co.uk

> These days, postcodes are used to determine whether or not an individual should receive a decent education, NHS operations or lifesaving drugs. In the case of pension annuities, postcodes could mean up to 10% more income for life.
>
> Source:  http://www.h-l.co.uk/news/feature-articles/pass-on-your-postcode---youre-not-properly-addressed-without-it

**Figure 6 – Pension Profiling Opportunity**

These examples illustrate that businesses create value judgements from the information input by their customers. They encourage us to share more information about ourselves in the hope that they may benefit from the relationships that our information can create.

Generic Social Graphing takes the same technical and analytical approach as the three examples above, but it differs in that it uses information that can be gathered for free or at low cost from published information. It does not depend upon, nor does it need, our collaboration. Any of our Digital Personality information can be used, irrespective of where it comes from or who posted it on the web.

Social Graphing and Profiling techniques are being used in a collaborative and in a generic way. The growth in the generic approach is one that we need to monitor. This is because historically the very practical safeguard to our personal privacy was the fragmented nature of paper based and unlinked digital information. Technology and Social Graphing techniques are fast eroding this safeguard.

## The issue of accuracy and relevance

The strength of Social Profiling and Graphing is the additional value generated by merging disparate datasets to create a picture that is more than the sum of its parts. A common issue inherent in merging data is that some of the data may be wrong, obsolete or out of context.

Information that is out of context has a habit of causing problems for individuals, especially where the organisation holding the information has the advantage of power or authority.

Consider the well-publicised example of Stacy Snyder where a photograph intended for use in a social context was recycled into a totally unrelated work context.

It is worth noting that the information that caused Stacey's problems was a photograph. Many libraries are now in the process of digitising their paper records, especially photographic records. This case could easily have been caused by a digitised paper based record.

> **"Woman Denied Degree Over 'Drunken Pirate" Myspace Photo Sues School"**
>
> Stacy Snyder, a twenty five year old senior at the university, posted a photograph of herself wearing a pirate hat while drinking from a "Mr. Goodbar" cup at a Halloween party. Snyder's advisor saw the photo and contacted her and student advisor, J. Barry Girvin, concerning the content of it. The claim was that the photograph was unprofessional and was "promoting underage drinking" even though she herself was well over the legal drinking age.
>
> The university denied Snyder her teaching degrees, maintaining that the reasons were due to poor "academic performance", not due to the posted photograph, and gave her a Bachelors of Arts in English. Two years later, Snyder is suing the school for denying her degree unjustly.
>
> Source:http://www.kirkarts.com/wiki/index.php?title=CMC:Peer_Wi ki_-_MySpace-FaceBook_2
>
> And:http://www.podcastingnews.com/content/2007/12/myspace-party-pic-cost-stacy-snyder-job/

**Figure 7 - Stacey Snyder**

Another more recent UK example occurred when Rebecca Posoli-Cilli found that an historic incident with a previous employer resurrected itself. Due to the nature of the incident, and the lack of any other available digital material in her search results, it came to dominate her Digital Personality and very nearly destroyed her new business. This illustrates the need to monitor the information that others are posting about us. In this case it was out of context, incomplete and negative information legitimately posted on the web as a routine part of her former employers process.

Rebecca Posoli-Cilli is the president of Freestream Aircraft, a private jet dealer. In a business like this a good reputation, especially online, is vital.

But misinformation on the internet nearly cost her her business.

When Ms Posoli-Cilli left her former job, before setting up the new company, her old employers were less than impressed and proceeded to sue her. She counter-sued, and the matter was settled out of court, a result she was very happy with.

She could have been forgiven for thinking that the matter was now settled.

In the brave new world of the internet, where every comment, photo and errant tweet can follow you indefinitely, things have a nasty habit of popping up again.

When prospective clients looked her up on Google, she says, details of the case popped up on that all-important first page.

"All you saw was this docket, that I'd been sued. But it didn't tell the whole story, it comes up as a black mark, but it didn't talk about the settlement."

Ms Posoli-Cilli's customers are among the wealthiest consumers in the world. They rarely appear on commercially available mailing lists, and they value their security and privacy. So this was potentially devastating.

One firm stopped doing business with her, despite a good working relationship.

Source: http://www.bbc.co.uk/news/business-12489632

**Figure 8 –Rebecca Posoli-Cilli**

A special burden can be placed upon the accuracy of information when organisations use it for approving financial transactions. The popularity of CreditExpert.co.uk[14] emphasises this concern.

The following quotes are taken from CreditExpert's own website explaining their role in correcting errors on behalf of their customers. It illustrates the impact of bad data upon their own customers profiles.

---

"I initially signed up as had been refused for a store card. I was able to find out why and have been able to monitor my financial status ever since - including adding a correction to an account which had false information. This increased my rating to a great rate and I have been monitoring it ever since. - Sally, Derby"

"Within hours of signing up, I was able to see quickly and easily my financial status and the depth of information stored about me was amazing. It was interesting to note the linked institutions and more recently, I have been able to quickly identify the parts of my finances to put in order to rectify my current situation. - Paul, Bicester"

Source:https://www.creditexpert.co.uk/order1_1.aspx?sc=410006& areaid=22&pkgid=UKMON&SiteID=100002&SiteVersionID=487&bcd =interactivehomepage1 24 June 2010

---

**Figure 9 - Credit Expert Website**

It is interesting to note that the CreditExpert business is successfully charging customers to use a tool to correct financial information errors that should not be on their database in the first place. It is an exceptional

---

[14] CreditExpert.com is a website whose primary purpose is to enable individuals to check the accuracy of their own Experian Credit Report.

business model that can persuade customers to pay for mistakes!

The fact that some people are prepared to pay to correct the errors in their data emphasises the importance of information accuracy to all of us.

We are producing so much information about ourselves and about so many other people and their activities, that our exposure to problems of inaccuracy and misinterpretation is a daily risk.

**Is this the future?**

The short answer is <u>yes</u>. Social Graphing is becoming a pre-requisite of a well-structured information based society. The identification and verification of individuals is a concern for us all. We need some method to be sure that the person we are communicating with is genuine.

The question of identity on the internet is being addressed by academics and businesses. FIDIS (The Future of Identity in the Information Society) is a European funded academic group created specifically to consider solutions to this issue. Their work is primarily concerned with confirming identity, rather than analysing personality, but the techniques used and issues addressed have huge overlaps.

> Digitising personal information is changing our ways of identifying persons and managing relations. What used to be a 'natural' identity is now as virtual as a user account at a web portal, an email address, or a mobile phone number. It is subject to diverse forms of identity management in business, administration, and among citizens.
>
> A core question and source of conflict is who owns how much identity information of whom and who needs to place trust into which identity information to allow access to resources.
>
> Source: FIDIS Summit Book: The Future of Identity in the Information Society - Challenges and Opportunities

**Figure 10 - FIDIS on Identification**

The quote above from a 2010 FIDIS summit highlights the issues as currently perceived by academics. These are:

- The idea of virtual identity becoming the first impression.

- Ownership of the information is in doubt.

- The concept of trust in a digital world is becoming fundamental.

This leads us to another question. Once we have established whom we are dealing with, how can we distinguish the important information from the frivolous or misleading?

The following quote is a short excerpt from a 2008 comprehensive academic analysis of the subject of digital identity. It leads us to a conclusion that Social

Profiling and Graphing will eventually become essential.

---

In the eyes of many, one of the most challenging problems of the information society is that we are faced with an ever expanding mass of information.

Selection of the relevant bits of information seems to become more important than the retrieval of data as such: the information is all out there, but what it means and how we should act on it may be one of the big questions of the 21st century.

If an information society is a society with an exponential proliferation of data, a knowledge society must be the one that has learned how to cope with this.

Profiling technologies seem to be one of the most promising technological means to create order in the chaos of proliferating data.

Source: Profiling the European Citizen Cross-Disciplinary Perspectives - Hildebrandt, Mireille; Gutwirth, Serge (Eds.); 2008, ISBN 978-1-4020-6913-0

---

**Figure 11 – Profiling Technologies**

In conclusion, unless we can establish a reliable method of identifying one another, society may never reap the real benefits of mass online communication and transaction processing. This is because the growth in the availability of personal information is driven by our own (and our contacts') actions and by commercial necessity. Both rely upon accurate identification of each party involved.

The available raw information about us is increasing, and the development of profiling techniques is facilitating this increase by linking previously disparate data.

There is little planned intent in all this; it is just a consequence of what we all do when we go online. Information sharing is becoming as natural as talking or letter writing in the pre-digital age.

The risks and opportunities created by all this personal data are rooted in how others perceive and use the data. It is for this reason that we must pay attention to our Digital Personality.

Key questions we can ask include:

- Will analysis techniques such as Social Graphing reveal any inconsistencies between different parts of my own Digital Personality and those of my wider network of contacts?

- Are there any errors or negatives in the raw information that is available about me?

- What is my Digital Personality saying to others who are meeting me for the first time?

In the next chapter, I will show how others affect our own Digital Personality. This also gives us some insight into how others may initially see us.

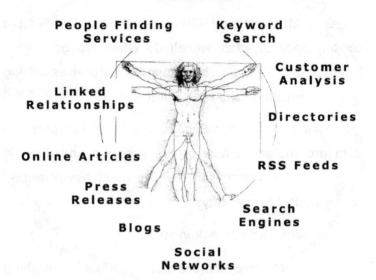

Digitised
Paper Media

People Finding
Services

Keyword
Search

Customer
Analysis

Linked
Relationships

Directories

Online Articles

RSS Feeds

Press
Releases

Blogs

Search
Engines

Social
Networks

# What others say about us

# is important.

# How Others Affect Us

## A little information can go a long way

Each time additional information about us becomes available for others to use, it has the potential to create a richer picture of who we are. This is because businesses are routinely sharing data with their partner organisations, which then use this information for authentication, operational and marketing purposes.

This is not illegal, nor is it necessarily a problem. Many businesses are already sharing information about us with their business partners. It is legitimate and necessary for their operations and there are laws, reviewed elsewhere in this book, that govern how they can use personal information.

The aspect of information sharing that I want to explore is not a legal or privacy issue, although these are clearly potential concerns. I am interested in how the use and recycling of information about us tends to expand our Digital Personality. Every time data about us is linked to a new database, it has the potential to reveal further aspects of our identity.

PayPal[15] is a leading online payment service provider that is setting one of the best examples in publicising the data sharing aspect of their business. They disclose the list of organisations with which they share information. This is included in full in Appendix 1 as a model of a clear and helpful format.

The following abbreviated list was extracted from their website in November 2010.[16] It is from a longer general notice that informs us that they have made some changes to their terms and conditions.

---

The PayPal Privacy Policy allows PayPal to disclose certain PayPal customer information to additional third parties as follows:

Convergys Customer Management Group Inc. (UK)
Equifax Plc (UK), CRIBIS D&B S.r.l. (Italy).
Bürgel Wirtschaftsinformationen GmbH & Co. KG (Germany)
PrePay Technologies Limited (trading as PrePay Solutions) (UK)
Trustwave (US)
Northstar Research Partners (USA)
Text 100 AB (Sweden)
Satmetrix Systems, Inc. (USA)
Acxiom France (France)
Adelanto (France)
Consultix (France and Spain) and Quadro Srl (Italy)
Blue Media S.A. (Poland)
Consultix GmbH (Germany)

Source: See Appendix 1

---

**Figure 12 – PayPal's Information Sharing Terms**

---

[15] See - www.PayPal.com
[16]https://cms.paypal.com/uk/cgi-bin/marketingweb?cmd=_render-content&fli=true&content_ID=ua/upcoming_policies_full&locale.x=en_GB

It is included here to illustrate the extent to which organisations share our data with their business partners. We should note several things:

- This list represents the changes to the PayPal policy agreement made in late 2010. This is only a partial picture showing amendments. The full listing of data sharing with partner organisations is published elsewhere on their website. There is not enough space in this book to recreate that list.

- The list indicates how the partner organisations will use the shared information. Thirteen organisations are listed and the majority of these businesses are there to generate marketing opportunities for PayPal. These organisations will probably apply Social Profiling and Graphing techniques to the personal information shared by PayPal.

- The list is part of the default general terms and conditions for the website. Customers accept all the conditions when using their services. PayPal could allow customers to fine tune the decision to share information, but they do not. It seems that there are at least two reasons for sharing information. These are operational necessities and marketing opportunities. Perhaps customers could have the option to opt out of the marketing?

- The details in the list make no mention of the level of sharing that the PayPal partner organisations will allow with their own, second level, partner organisations. Neither does it offer any reassurance that there are any restrictions upon how the data is shared with their second level partners. Therefore, we have to assume that the information can and will be shared onwards many times, each time perhaps, for a slightly different use. The danger here is that subsets of the information will be used out of context. The dangers inherent in using information in that way are discussed in Chapter 2.

We should note that full marks must go to PayPal for being a market leader in their openness about information sharing policies. See Appendix 1.

When we have information, we can act upon it and I have included some of the practical things that we can do to manage our Digital Personality in chapter five.

## Sometimes businesses make mistakes

In November 2009 T-Mobile,[17] a major mobile communications company, discovered that staff had been selling the contact and contract details of their customers to third parties. This led to many T-Mobile customers receiving unexpected telephone marketing calls from rival phone suppliers. These calls occurred immediately before the expiry of the existing contract with T-Mobile and were attempts to persuade customers to switch to a new supplier.

---

[17] http://www.t-mobile.com/

Reports have been made that staff from T-Mobile passed customer details to third party brokers.

A report by BBC News claimed that the details of thousands of customers were passed on with brokers selling the data on to other phone firms who then cold-called the customers as their contracts were due to expire.

A spokesman for T-Mobile told said that the sale of the data had been 'deeply regrettable' and that it had been asked to keep it secret to avoid any criminal prosecutions being prejudiced.

He told BBC News: "T-Mobile takes the protection of customer information seriously. When it became apparent that contract renewal information was being passed on to third parties without our knowledge, we alerted the Information Commissioner's Office."

He continued by saying that T-Mobile and the Information Commissioners Officer (ICO) were working together and had identified the source of the breach, and that T-Mobile had 'proactively supported the ICO to help stamp out what is a problem for the whole industry'.

Commenting, commissioner Christopher Graham said the data breach was the biggest of its kind .......... Customers absolutely have the right to ask them whether or not their personal data is safe."

Steve Moyle, CTO of leading database security provider Secerno, said: ".......... In the digital age, your data is worth money, and people who are on the inside of the corporate firewall are not immune from theft.

"The second issue around this breach is the paltry sums that the offenders will be charged from violating the Data Security Act. The culprits will be charged thousands of pounds, which is not high enough to be a deterrent. The fines need to match the severity of the crime and to re-enforce the notion that stealing a person's information is a crime. These current fine amounts are not enough to do that, and the proof will come from the affected customers, who are likely to agree."

Source:      http://www.scmagazineuk.com/t-mobile-criticised-by-information-commissioner-after-rogue-employee-passes-on-customer-details-to-third-parties/article/157940/

**Figure 13 - T-Mobile Breaks the Rules**

This had a number of repercussions for the T-Mobile business, amongst others:

- The initial loss of business to rival phone contract suppliers.

- Adverse publicity and a loss of reputation in the marketplace.

- Further loss of business once the story hit the headlines.

The T-Mobile news story quoted above gives some idea of the media storm that followed the leak of information. There are several issues to note here:

- T-Mobile approached the UK Information Commissioner voluntarily. The impact of the subsequent publicity, in the form of negative media coverage, did not reflect their apparent honesty and integrity in dealing with this matter. This does not encourage others to be as open next time.

- Nobody from T-Mobile was quoted in the article; this makes me doubt the "ownership" of this problem within their organisation. Would it have been a career limiting decision to own this problem? If so, this culture will not encourage "whistleblowers" to highlight poor data management practices in the future.

- The news of the leak had been kept secret by mutual agreement with the authorities involved. This continued for some time to avoid prejudicing any criminal prosecutions. Does this mean that in some way punishing the few is more important than protecting the many? This seems to undervalue the immediate needs and rights of customers whose information has been misused.

● At the time of this incident the fines that the Information Commissioner could levy were disproportionately low in comparison to the seriousness of this infringement of The Data Protection Act. The limit on fines subsequently changed in 2010, but it does illustrate the historic misunderstanding amongst legislators about the seriousness of the consequences of personal data misuse.

This leaves us with a final question. To what degree will these underlying attitudes change in future to favour customers over the organisations that use data about them?

Has anything changed following the 2009 case at T-Mobile?

The following article summarises a 2010 survey by the Information Commissioners Office[18] regarding employee knowledge of the Data Protection Act. It records that knowledge is improving and it seems that in 2010 private sector companies were lagging behind the public sector in their knowledge of data protection.

---

[18] The Information Commissioner's Office is the UK's independent authority set up to uphold information rights in the public interest, promoting openness by public bodies and data privacy for individuals. - http://www.ico.gov.uk/

Research by the Information Commissioner's Office (ICO) found that overall awareness of five of the eight data protection principles increased between 2009 and 2010, but levels of awareness are still higher in the public sector than among private sector organisations.

The research, undertaken by SMSR on behalf of the ICO, found that just under half of private sector firms said, unprompted, that they should store personal information securely, compared with 60 per cent of public sector organisations.

Chris McIntosh, CEO of Stonewood[19] said that he found the statistic about private businesses still not grasping the Data Protection Act was 'shocking'.

He said: "Businesses need to reflect on the consequences of this failure to understand the Data Protection Act as they hold copious amounts of valuable personal data. In fact the average monetary value alone of data contained on a laptop is half a million pounds. Beyond this, businesses can and have lost large contracts as a result of data loss.

"To deal with this attitude, the ICO really needs to stick with its promises and finally start levelling appropriate fines. When it comes to securing personal data it's obvious that actions say more than a thousand words."

Source: http://www.scmagazineuk.com/public-sector-companies-embrace-data-protection-better-than-those-in-the-public-sector-according-to-ico-survey/article/190228/

**Figure 14 - A Regulatory Response**

It would appear that some progress is being made, but it is slow and it is being led by the public sector. Reading between the lines, the private sector may not understand the issue, or perhaps may not care too much.

---

[19] http://www.stonewood.co.uk/ - a world leader in the design, manufacture and support of data encryption products and services.

Ask yourself, can I name any of the eight data protection principles, or do I know the name of the data protection officer for the part of the organisation in which I work? If your answers included a "No" then the survey above is referring to you and/or your organisation.

Most of us do not understand the question until it is too late, when something has gone wrong.

**Organisations change the rules**

Personal information is generally benign when used in context and in an appropriate time period. In the paper world, as time passed the data about us disappeared, either shredded or filed into an archive that took time and effort to access. Digital data can be, and often is, kept forever. This data can be reprocessed through different systems and processes, often at the touch of a button.

This is just what happened to Members of UK Parliament in 2009/10.

The UK Parliament expenses scandal has given us a glimpse of what can happen when old data is subject to retrospective changes of the rules. Many MPs had been claiming expenses and were assured by the system that this was legitimate. The internal governance mechanism had approved their claims.

---

The Daily Telegraph newspaper in the UK used leaked information to publish expenses claims that Members of Parliament had thought were private and that had been approved within their own long established rules.

As all the payments had been approved by the appropriate authorities, there was no reason for MP's working within the rules to have any concerns.

When this system was exposed to public scrutiny it caused immense problems for those involved. After a short inquiry, the rules were retrospectively changed and actions that MP's assumed would remain hidden came back to haunt them.

Many were forced to resign or to repay expenses that were claimed many years earlier.

It cost the careers of many MP's.

---

**Figure 15 - The Effect of Retrospective Rule Changes**

Then, following the leak of information to the Daily Telegraph, the rules were retrospectively changed.

This illustrates why, in future, we might want to exercise more control over how our own personal data is stored and used.

Public opinion at the time supported the Daily Telegraph, and this somehow justified the leak of the data from Parliament. This justification was driven by public outrage at the excesses of some of the MPs expenses claims, not by any concern for good information management.

The points that were never adequately debated in public were:

- Everyone is innocent until proven guilty and is entitled to privacy in their dealings with their "employer". This case begins to undermine this principle for us all.

- The data leak was a serious breach of confidence that was somehow justified by the need for the public to know the details.

- The original system that approved the expenses payments was nullified and retrospective rules were applied in their place. The acceptance by Parliament of a retrospective change of the rules seems counter to our sense of order and structure. If our actions are within the law, but can be made "illegal" at a future date, it may be best that we do not allow too much to be recorded.

This case shows that in the digital age, old, "hidden" information can be quickly resurrected. Information can also be speedily reprocessed against any new set of criteria.

**Sometimes businesses are careless**

In 2009, Research conducted by Fellowes[20] showed that 79% of businesses make no effort to destroy the

---

[20] http://www.fellowes.com an international specialist supplier of document management equipment and systems.

sensitive material that they throw away or are preparing to recycle.

> ........Shockingly, only 64% of businesses have put in place a clear policy on how to handle documents with sensitive information - which no doubt goes some way to explaining why nearly one-third (32%) of employees admit to always throwing sensitive documents directly into the bin!
> The 97% of employees are therefore justified in their beliefs that their company does not completely protects customers' identities; furthermore, 64% of employees believe that bins are a bigger risk to customer details than computer systems or document theft
> Overall, 71% of UK employees think their companies should do more to ensure confidential documents are handled responsibly - and the UK is not alone. 66% of German, 70% of Belgian, 61% of Dutch and 85% of Irish employees agree that more should be done........
>
> Source: http://blog.stop-idfraud.co.uk/2009/10/it-could-be-you.php#more

**Figure 16 – Fellowes Data Security Survey**

It can be argued that attitudes to, and awareness of, personal information usage has improved in the last half of the past decade. There is a growing awareness of the importance of data security in both government and non-government organisations. We can see this in the output from some government departments, in their staff guidance and best practices publications.[21] A good summary of the type of protection mandated by the UK Government is published annually by the Cabinet office.

---

[21] http://www.cabinetoffice.gov.uk/media/207318/hmg_security_policy.pdf

This points to a general improvement in the security of our personal information, but the motivation for this increased awareness is polarised between two different drivers.

- First, is the embarrassment and reputation damage to an organisation caused when information is leaked or lost. The T-Mobile example earlier in this chapter illustrates this point well. They were apologetic and co-operative, but ultimately the financial loss was in terms of lost business, not statutory fines.

- Second, the potential for litigation can arise when an organisation retains too much information. Many organisations keep minimal records because a demand for legal disclosure of information could reveal more than they wish. When organisations keep too much information they incur the costs of reviewing thousands files prior to disclosure and this is prohibitive. Therefore as a defensive measure, it can sometimes pay to keep minimal records.

It appears that the recent general improvement in information management and security are partly driven by the desire for organisations to protect themselves from the risks of careless management. Improvements are not driven by altruistic concerns for our personal information.

Figure 16 above reports upon the frequent casual attitudes towards data security encountered by the Fellowes survey. We can test this for ourselves by asking this simple question.

"Do I and my colleagues always securely destroy files which contain personal identifiers as soon as we have finished with them, or do they languish on our system until we can find time to do our electronic housekeeping?"

If like me, you are only human, you will generally put off the digital housekeeping until a later date. Sometimes I never do it at all. It is just the way we are as human beings.

## Businesses aggregate information

Harvesting personal data from social networking sites is not currently an infringement of intellectual property rights, nor is it seen as an infringement of personal privacy. Given the synergistic value of aggregated personal information, and the ability to link anonymous personal data to other databases, it is surprising that the ownership of harvested information is rarely questioned.

In summary, businesses buy, sell, harvest and aggregate personal information for their own commercial uses.

There are guidelines and legal penalties relating to how they should handle personal information and what they can expect if they break the rules.

However, recent examples show that their primary motivator is either profitability or the maintenance of their public reputation. It is unlikely that any business will automatically curtail its activities out of concern for an individual Digital Personality.

This is ironic, because every time an organisation manipulates your personal information they will be linking you to another dataset, and in doing so they are building another branch of your Digital Personality.

**Lack of understanding about new things invokes fear.**

# Our Psychological Reaction

Digital networking is driving two conflicting attitudes about privacy:

- When others have access to our personal information, we fear that we may be losing our privacy. This makes us feel less safe.

- We want to identify others with a high degree of certainty before we enter into a transaction with them. This makes us feel much safer.

For the first, we want to reveal the minimum about ourselves. For the second, conversely, we want others to reveal as much as possible.

This conflict is fed to us everyday. There are constant stories about leaks, identity theft, hacking and poor standards of information management in government and big business. This fear is compounded by the increasing penetration of internet-enabled devices in new locations. The ubiquity of this technology makes it appear that we are being tracked, monitored and recorded wherever we go.

Our need to know more about others comes from our desire to participate and benefit from the emerging internet technologies. In the last ten years we have seen the emergence of wikis, blogs, video sharing, picture hosting, collaboration tools, eCommerce, social networks and online data storage. We are pulled into this world by the convenience of the systems. In some cases we are now obliged to use online tools as the only way to transact with organisations. To do so we need to trust the person with whom we are transacting. To trust them we must have a way to identify them with certainty.

Clearly, to be successful in the digital world we need to move away from ingrained attitudes about maintaining and guaranteeing privacy, towards surrendering some privacy in order to be able to participate. This means moving away from protecting our Digital Personality and towards managing it.

The old attitudes are about avoidance. This is driven by negative fears about impersonation, reputation and fraud. The reporting mechanisms that we rely upon in this old world are reactive. They tell us when our fears have been realised. You discover someone is using your identity, you see something that has been written about you in a blog or the bank calls to ask if you have used your credit card recently. Our gut reaction is that we want to stop it, avoid it and prevent it.

The new attitudes will be about concern for efficiency. This is a proactive reaction to the dangers of impersonation, reputation damage and fraud and we need tools to help us manage the dangers. These tools will detect impersonation and comment upon the impersonators, manage and promote our reputations and detect fraud and track its resolution.

As these tools emerge, a key factor in their success will be the degree of trust that we place in the organisations and people who provide them. The following quote from the author Margaret Atwood neatly expresses exactly this potential barrier.

---

I am sceptical about people (not technology sic). The nature of the tool can change how we live – for instance, I'm sitting here at 6am in Toronto talking to you over broadband. In earlier eras, I would have written something in cuneiform on wet clay and had it delivered to you on horseback.

The tool is morally neutral. It's not a case of 'is science telling us the truth, or is technology bad?' I'm more sceptical about human nature.

Who is in charge of those tools?

Who is putting those CCTV cameras up all over the UK?

Whose hands are on the tools?"

Source: 2010 BBC Radio 4 interview with Margaret Atwood, Author.

---

**Figure 17 - A Comment on Trust**

## Who can we trust?

There are a number of UK organisations that are forming public opinion in this area. These include No2ID[22], Campaign for Freedom of Information[23] and Liberty[24].

Quotes from the home pages of their websites are shown below. The language used is instructive.

> NO2ID is a campaigning organisation. We are a single-issue group focussed on the threat to liberty and privacy posed by the rapid growth of the database state.
>
> If you believe Britain is too secretive a society, please support our work by making a donation. Your contribution will make a difference.
>
> Liberty campaigns to protect basic rights and freedoms through the courts, in Parliament and in the wider community.

**Figure 18 - Privacy Campaigners**

The dialogue here stresses the concern about privacy; there is little emphasis on the effectiveness of sharing information. Their communications and messages have stressed that the public _should_ care about privacy, more recently the language has changed to emphasise that we _need to_ care and to act. This reflects a growing awareness that privacy is being

---

[22] www.no2id.net/
[23] www.cfoi.org.uk/
[24] http://www.liberty-human-rights.org.uk

eroded. Do we care enough to act and have we the tools to do so? It seems that society will have to learn to care because we are beginning to recognise that online transactions are here to stay. We cannot avoid them.

Most of the dialogue around privacy simplifies the trust / privacy message into a "one size fits all" argument. i.e. The people with the information are powerful because they have it. Power corrupts and therefore we cannot trust them.

When campaigning groups are telling us that we cannot trust the large organisations of state and big business with our data the language that they use to communicate the message is fear based. Using loaded terms such as privacy and identity increases our unease.

The world is more subtle than this. Trust is never a black and white issue. There is always some risk in all transactions. Attitudes to trust relate to who is using our information and for what purpose. The type of organisation and type of person involved is the key.

Therefore, I think we need a societal change in the language that is used and more effective, user-friendly tools to track the use of personal information held by organisations.

Furthermore, the businesses that are at the forefront of the development of these tools will find themselves in a powerful position of trust with their existing and potential customers.

### Moving from mistrust to trust

When we mistrust we are fearful. When we trust we will participate. In between there is a sort of neutral area where we neither mistrust nor trust the organisation holding our information. This neutral no-man's-land is a place where there is no fear, but there is also no participation.

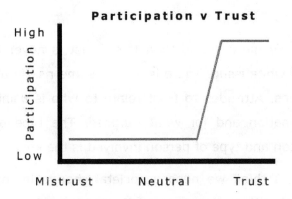

Figure 19 - From Mistrust To Trust

For us to participate we need to trust an organisation; *absence of mistrust* is not enough.

Organisations will need to address the reduction of our mistrust before we can start to trust them enough to participate fully in their digital business processes; and active participation is essential for us all to benefit from the efficiencies of services delivered using new technology.

Mistrust will be lessened when it is easier for us to find out what information organisations are holding about us. The ability to comment upon the information or to ask for amendments may be a future prerequisite for this to happen.

Trust will be increased when we can see the decisions being made with the information held. Our fear comes from the unknown and it goes away when we have the ability to see fair processing and outcomes.

This is simply a matter of organisations recognising that when convenience outweighs our concerns we will then participate. Removing our concerns is a prerequisite to enabling our trust in technology led convenience.

Those of us who are active internet users or who have made an online purchase can no longer avoid our

Digital Personality and hope it will go away. We must embrace it, because it is here by default, through our own actions and the actions of others.

**Figure 20 – Convenience vs Concern**

Our desire for convenience is creating a Digital Personality by default. We need to start thinking about managing it or it will continue to develop by itself.

As consumers, we also need to recognise and encourage any organisations that provide the tools to help us to manage our personal data.

Blank Page

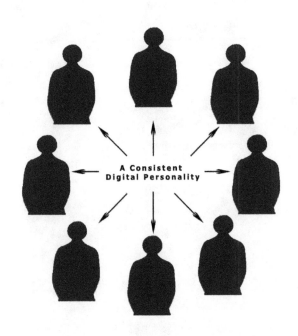

**How can we manage our dispersed digital personalities?**

# Management Strategies

## Three options

We can choose from three options for a strategy for managing our Digital Personality. They are not mutually exclusive.

- Do nothing.
- React to what we see.
- Proactively manage.

## Option 1 - Do nothing

According to the results of my own short survey of students at Cambridge University in 2010, there are real benefits to being available online. These results reflect the attitudes of a born digital generation. They include:

- Being in the loop. It is the only way to know what is going on.

- Being open. This encourages others to contact us, to converse. The more contacts you have the better connected you are both socially and academically.

- Being visible. A lack of visibility is suspicious. We have no idea who you are. This is especially relevant in a community where openness and visibility are seen as positive attributes

Many over 40s are actively following the do nothing strategy. They would prefer that the idea of Digital Personality did not exist. It makes them very uncomfortable.

Doubtless, some younger people are following this strategy too. It is the classic early stage reaction to change, well documented by Kubler Ross[25] and others. When a change happens, we generally deny that it affects us, we do not need it, we deny that others need it and, very often, we will ridicule the change as a coping strategy.

To anyone in this group I would recommend that you wait and see. Try to sense what others are publishing on your behalf; keep an eye upon the amount of information that is appearing about you. Others are already creating your Digital Personality and it is in your interests to know what they are doing.

Try to understand what the younger members of your family or work group are doing online. Why do they

---

[25] The Kubler Ross Change Curve. The stages are commonly listed as Shock, Denial, Fear, Anger, Depression, Understanding, Acceptance and Action – Elizabeth Kubler-Ross, On Death and Dying, Pub Macmillan 1969.

communicate and share in this way? What benefit do they get from it?

Common arguments for people of this opinion are:

- Virtual communication is not as effective as face-to-face conversations.

- Putting personal information online is risky. Identity theft and fraud are real and widespread risks. i.e. The more I have out there the more likely it is to happen. This attitude is encouraged by businesses trying to sell us security tools.

- It is time consuming; I already have email and online shopping etc. to cope with. This is just another distraction.

- FaceBook is only for kids.

If you find yourself sympathising with these statements then you might need to think carefully about what others are creating on your behalf.

- Is your CV being shared?

- What are your relatives posting online after family parties?

- What does your employer publish on their website, blog and social networking spaces?

These datasets will become your default personality if you do not try to influence them.

Finally, a default personality is not necessarily a bad thing. Others are not deliberately trying to create a bad profile for you, but as the saying goes; "one man's meat is another man's poison". As we have seen in the case of Stacey Snyder in Chapter 2, whilst it is acceptable for some people to appear online holding a glass of beer, it may not be for others. Trusting others' judgements in these matters is not a way to control your Digital Personality.

**Option 2 - React to what we see**

This strategy is reactive. It recognises that we live in a world where others can influence our Digital Personalities. We need to make sure that we control and manage what others are saying.

Those in this group understand the concept of a Digital Personality but have not yet recognised that it has its advantages. They see only the downside disadvantages. In terms of the Kubler Ross change model, they have probably reached the Anger or the Understanding stage. They see Digital Personality only as a potential inconvenience.

There are some useful tools available to reduce the amount of information published about us, but this strategy could be time consuming.

As a starting point, I recommend that you search for yourselves on Google, Yahoo! or Bing search engines. This is what others will do when they want to find out more about you. Try to imagine what words they would link to you in a search. For example, "Adam Blackie AND Information Manager" is what I would like others to think of when they search for me. In fact, this is probably not the case, so ask a few friends what they think. How would they sum you up in two or three words? If nothing else, this is an interesting game to play over dinner or a beer in a bar.

Always use the phrases that others mention, as these are the words that tell you what others will find when they look for you online. In this context, what others think about you is far more important than what you think about yourself.

At a slightly more sophisticated level, you could also try a regular search at Pipl.com.[26]

| Pipl Search Criteria |
| --- |
| Name, City, State, Country, email, Screen Names (used in Online forums etc), Phone Numbers and Business Name. |

**Figure 21 – Pipl.com Search Criteria**

---

[26] www.Pipl.com

This online directory allows you to search for information about yourself in more detail and at a deeper level than Google, Yahoo! etc.

The Pipl.com search criteria are, as the name suggests, more focussed on finding people. They also claim to list information not indexed by the mainstream search engines.

The results of a search on www.Pipl.com will take around ten minutes to complete as each criteria is searched separately. Then you have to trawl through the results to see who is saying what about you. I am relatively atypical in that I have an unusual name. Most people, with more popular names, will find pages and pages of information. This takes time and needs a regular review – say every three months.

You could also subscribe to online reputation management services such as Reputation Defender[27].

---

**The Reputation Defender Strap Line**

Learn how to improve your online privacy and reputation, and how to control what's in your search results.

**Figure 22 – ReputationDefender.com**

---

[27] www.reputationdefender.com

These services have a variety of methods and tools to help automate the search and removal of personal information on the web. Reputation Defender focuses upon removing negativity from your Digital Personality.

**What do I do next?**

So, you searched the web and found all sorts of personal information. You may not be responsible for it being there, but you now want I removed. What can you do?

We do not have any firm legal rights to proactively manage our personal information. The reason for this is explained in more depth in the next chapter of this book.

I can recommend several approaches that I have found useful. These are suggestions that really do work in the real world.

Write and ask the holder of the information to either delete or make the information anonymous. The key is to be polite and specific and to provide the key information that identifies you to be the person to whom the information relates. An example communication is included in Appendix 2.

The most effective strategy is to send requests via an email, duplicated in a letter. Occasionally big corporations ignore the email whereas a well-worded letter, perhaps arriving via registered post, often receives more attention. This is because letters are a relative rarity compared to the volume of emails they receive.

In either case be prepared for silence for a period. The notion that they should delete information because it is about you will be a new concept to most organisations. The conventional wisdom is that the information belongs to them. Why would you take an interest in it?

Two motivators prompt organisational action:

- First, is your attitude to direct marketing. Being clear that you never want to receive any communication from them again removes any value they may derive from keeping your data.

- Second, is the heightened risk that a misuse or leak of your personal information carries, particularly if the organisation has previously declined your request to delete it.

Be prepared for a "can't do that" type response. It is a fact that many organisations do not have a delete option for their databases. The best they can do is to make it anonymous, and in some cases where your name and address are key database fields they will not be able to do this either.

There are some other ways that you can target organisations that hold your personal information. These are organisations where the sharing of information is routine practice. Either you have a choice about whether you want to share your information, or there are established ways to request its deletion.

Here are a number of specific things to do if you want to use the "react to what I see" strategy:

- NHS Central Patient Records - you will need to write to your GP if you want him or her to put a "stop" on your records being uploaded to the NHS "spine" automatically. There are potential consequences of doing this. Your details will not be available to GPs if you are ill away from home. You need to decide if this is a risk you are prepared to take.

- FaceBook – to search FaceBook you will need to be a member. If you are not a member, ask a friend who is a member to search for you. Anything visible to that person will generally be visible to all. You can then contact the owners of tagged images and ask them to remove them. However, there is no obligation to do so and appealing to FaceBook support staff will be your final resort. If you have a FaceBook account make sure you understand the privacy settings for your account. There is plenty of help available from other users.

● For an organisation that you know holds information about you - make a subject access request (see Appendix 3). Their response will tell you what information the organisation holds about you and from their reply you should be able to work out why. If you do not believe they have a valid reason for holding on to your information, ask them to delete it.

● When you become aware that an organisation holds your personal information, you can simply make an Information Deletion request (see Appendix 2). These are not binding upon the organisation, which has no legal obligation to comply, but I have found that they work well. The motivation is twofold. First, organisations like to be responsive as they can easily generate adverse publicity if they refuse too many requests. Second, how would it look if the database details were leaked or are stolen and they had previously refused to remove your details? This would appear doubly negligent. It is also best to send a letter not an email. The response rate is higher.

● Opting out of the version of the Electoral Role that local authorities sell to marketers. This is called "The Edited Register". You can either tick the box on the electoral registration form when it comes around in the autumn or send a simple letter to your local authority requesting that they remove your details from this version. See Appendix 4.

● Cancel any Shopping Loyalty cards that you have. Retailers are the most common collectors and users of your information. Once you have done this write to them to ask them to delete your information. See Appendix 2.

● Use cash for smaller shop purchases. Every credit and debit card transaction is logged by the card provider, and the information is automatically shared with a variety of organisations. Note that there are also obvious risks in carrying too much cash.

● Register for the Mailing Preference Service.[28] It prevents direct mailing companies from using your mailing address. This preference can be overridden by the small print in any contract that you sign with individual organisations. So watch out for this in any new transaction.

● Register for the Telephone Preference Service.[29] It prevents telephone sales companies from using your telephone numbers. This can be overridden by the small print in the contract that you sign with individual organisations. So watch out for this in any small print.

● You should delete any social media accounts that you no longer use. There are some interesting tools emerging that help to do this. Two that I will mention are Suicide Machine[30] and Delete Your Account[31]. The first claims to take all the effort out of deleting your old social network links on Facebook, Myspace, Twitter and LinkedIn. It

---

[28] www.mpsonline.org.uk/mpsr/mps_choosetype.html
[29] http://www.tpsonline.org.uk/ctps/number_type.html
[30] http://suicidemachine.org/
[31] http://deleteyouraccount.com/

guarantees deletion of all content, not just your account details. The other provides information about how to delete your account from all of the major social networking, blogging, shopping etc. sites and services across the web.

◦ When web browsing you need to know that some websites will store and use information on your computer. Cookies are the most common method. These are helpful in that they allow you to browse more quickly, but some of them automatically share information with their own databases. It would need an extra book to cover this topic in detail so you will have to research your own particular web browser and learn how to control the settings.

This strategy incurs a heavy workload in managing your Digital Personality because you must continually monitor your personal information exposure. You are attempting to limit the risk that the wrong sort of information will damage your reputation.

Preventing organisations from using and trading your personal information is the core strategy and your continued efforts alongside their voluntary co-operation will be the keys to its success.

## Option 3 - Proactively manage

This is without doubt my preferred option for managing your Digital Personality. The reason is that it is easier to achieve a satisfactory result. Options 1 and 2 allow others to take the proactive role in building your Digital Personality. This option is about creating a great Digital Personality for yourself and then proactively managing it.

The positive image that you create will be the one that people will find first, and they rarely go further than this. Social media profiles are highly ranked by search engines like Google, so making sure your positive information is promoted puts any negative information into context, pushing it farther down the search pages.

This addresses the long-term risks associated with your Digital Personality, because these are largely about reputation management. The Stacey Snyder case illustrates the point perfectly (see the second chapter on Social Profiling).

What this strategy recognises is the innate impatience of human beings. We want quick results and this explains why Google is so popular. It is quick, easy to use and makes a very convenient platform for online communication tools of all kinds.

The strategy exploits this human trait in the following way. If I search for Adam Blackie in Google and I see twenty results, all with the same look and feel, then I am content that Adam is a nice fellow and I will click on a few of the links there. If I am very curious, I might click on several links. It would be very unusual for me to spend any more time than this unless I was conducting a serious investigation into Adam Blackie's background. If I were a doing that I would probably use one of the specialist tools like Pipl.com or Reputation Defender or a search engine aggregator.[32]

What this strategy delivers is the creation of sufficient positive material about you to ensure that people searching for your information will be satisfied with what they first see. There are many ways to achieve this result.

A proactive strategy using current technology is outlined below, but this may change as other tools become available. It will also change depending upon the image you want to portray, how much effort you want to put in and what your peer group expects of you. The following strategy, once created, takes as little as an hour a week to maintain and it provides a positive, friendly and open image as well as inviting others to connect where appropriate. Most

---

[32] Search engine aggregators are tools that use search queries across the specialist search engines. The results are far more detailed.

importantly, it is what you want others to see when they search for you.

- FaceBook Account[33] – Limit this to very close friends and family. Exclude anyone who is not directly linked to you. Keep personal photos to a minimum because other people can recycle them. Make sure you monitor the information that relatives post to their accounts after parties and other events. You can un-tag photos that have your name attached, but you cannot delete them. Your relatives can delete them, so please ask. Keep comments friendly, informative and helpful. Think carefully before you hit the Enter key!

- LinkedIn Account[34] - Limit this to business use only. Few of the connections from here should appear on FaceBook or vice versa. The profile must be scrupulously honest, positive and professional. Never post a negative comment. Never link to negative people. Use a photo that represents how you want others to perceive you. Status updates will be about something you are researching (others may contribute) or about significant changes in your employment (others may be able to help).

- Twitter Account.[35] This is useful. Google likes Twitter. Have two accounts. One where you only post information that you feel will be useful to your

---

[33] www.facebook.com/adam.blackie?v=info – Adam Blackie's FaceBook profile. – Maximum Privacy
[34] http://uk.linkedin.com/in/adamblackie - Adam Blackie's LinkedIn profile – Maximum Openness
[35] http://twitter.com/#search?q=adamablackie – Adam Blackie's Twitter Account – Business Use Only – no Chatter

business contacts. It is about highlighting information that you have that others will find useful. It can be integrated into your LinkedIn account too. The second account is a personal account. You use it to communicate to friends and relatives. This strategy also needs two mobile phone numbers to be effective.

A blog[36]. This is a statement about who you are and what you do. It does not have to be regular nor does it have to be particularly original. One or two posts a year will do. Most blogs are so unpopular that the chances are that no one will read them anyway. The point is that it is another piece of positive internet content about you that will be shown when someone searches for your name.

Consider using a Gravatar.[37] This is a type of online business card that can be integrated into news and social networking websites. Their advantage is that if you change your Gravatar, it changes in all its locations across the web. You can maintain a consistent message in all the places where your picture or details appear.

My business has a simple static website that contains a brief description of what I do professionally. With basic free web design tools, this takes an afternoon to complete and publish. It is linked to all the other social media tools that I use. The links provide more information for web search engines to find and index. It is a useful

---

[36] http://adamblackie.wordpress.com – Adam Blackie's Blog – Simple business stuff, trying to be helpful.
[37] http://en.gravatar.com/adamblackie - Adam Blackie's Gravatar

spin-off that people who search for me should associate me with my work.

- Occasionally contribute positive and supportive comments to non-controversial discussions on reputable web sites such as the BBC, LinkedIn and WordPress. You could try a comment on my blog or a comment about this book on Amazon.com. These comments are visible to search engines and they provide a varied mix of search results when your name is used in search engines.

Essentially this strategy is relying upon the fact that the positive and deliberate content provided can push other information into the background. It is establishing the first impression that others have when they search online. First impressions count.

You may have to use this strategy alongside a little of the "React to what you see" strategy. When negative or conflicting items occasionally appear on your profile, it is possible to remove them by using techniques outlined in option 2. However with a more positive and proactive Digital Personality under your control most people will not see these conflicting items anyway.

**So, who owns the information about**

**Adam Blackie?**

# Are New Laws Needed?

In the UK, there is a great deal of legislation containing general and specific references to personal information handling. So, which elements of the law will help manage your Digital Personality?

In early 2010, as part of a wider project, I was commissioned by a client to produce a list of UK legislation where the subject of personal information handling appears. The list was huge and growing. We did not complete the task.

We found that most of the legislation includes several themes:

- Personal information can be held by organisations for a reasonable period of time, depending upon business needs.

- Personal information must be held securely and generally used only for the purpose for which it was collected.

- The individual to whom the information relates has some rights to ensure it is accurate.

It is interesting to note that none of the legislation specifically addresses ownership of personal information. The consensus is that the holding organisation is the owner and the person to whom it relates has limited influence over how and what is held.

To understand more about the extent of the influence we have on our personal data it is useful to review the most important pieces of UK legislation in this area, before coming to any conclusions.

**Data Protection Act (1998)**

The Data Protection Act 1998 gives you the right to apply for a copy of your personal information.

A request can be made in writing, by letter or email, and you send it to the person or organisation you believe holds information about you. A fee of up to £10.00 for each request may be made.

There are some issues here.

- There are a huge number of organisations that might be holding information about you. How do you know where to start?

- The cost of £10 per request could start to mount up if we were serious about this.

- A quick count of the organisations I have dealt with in the last year or so would keep me busy for a week or more.

It seems that this legislation may be good for remedying errors after they have occurred, but is not practical for ongoing management of your Digital Personality.

The Data Protection Act can help manage personal information
**Access information**
Find out what information is held about you on a computer and within some manual records.
**Correct information**
If you believe your personal data is inaccurate, you can write to the organisation to tell them what you believe is wrong with your information and what should be done to correct it.
**Prevent processing of information**
You can ask an organisation not to process information about you that causes substantial unwarranted damage or distress.
**Prevent unsolicited marketing**
An organisation is required not to process information about you for direct marketing purposes if you ask them not to.
**Prevent automated decision making**
In some circumstances you can object to organisations making significant decisions about you where the decision is completely automated and there is no human involvement.

Source: Extract from the ICO website[38]

**Figure 23 – The Data Protection Act (1998)**

## Freedom of Information Act (2000)

This act requires the disclosure of information held by public authorities or by persons providing services for them.

---

[38]www.ico.gov.uk/for_the_public/personal_information/how_manage.aspx

If you make a request for information to a public body, they should:

- Inform you in writing whether it holds information of the description specified in your request.

- Communicate the information to you.

There is usually no fee payable for the service, except where complying with your request incurs an unreasonable cost. This is increasingly being applied to complex requests.

There is also a clause that prevents frequent requests as follows:

> Where a public authority has previously complied with a request for information which was made by any person, it is not obliged to comply with a subsequent identical or substantially similar request from that person unless a reasonable interval has elapsed between compliance with the previous request and the making of the current request.
>
> Source – UK Govt Website [39]

**Figure 24 - FOI Act Exemption**

Therefore, the FOI act is useful because you can see the information that a government body holds about you, but they have no obligation to amend it, nor do they have to keep you repeatedly updated.

---

[39] www.legislation.gov.uk/ukpga/2000/36/section/14

It is relatively easy for an organisation to find an excuse to refuse a Freedom of Information (FOI) request.

This is not an active management tool for our Digital Personality.

**Public Records Act (1958)**

A public record is essentially a government record that has been selected for permanent preservation. This generally happens when a record is 30 years old, but can be earlier or later in some circumstances.

Public records include personal data. This is generally held in a "closed"[40] status until the subject of the information is deceased. In some cases, information is kept closed for longer periods to protect the privacy of the relatives of the deceased.

This is a very secure set of personal information. It is not likely that others can see information about you held under the Public Records Act. This is because the records are not fully electronically indexed yet. Presently the manual indices and electronic catalogues do not list individual names in documents unless they are historically significant. i.e. they relate to a VIP or

---

[40] Closed simply means that the public can not usually access the record in the Public Records Office

similar. Ordinary folk are left hidden in the file and finding this information is laborious.

Accessing personal information in Public Records can also be achieved by using the Freedom of Information Act provisions. However, you need to know that it exists before you ask for it. General search enquiries are not allowed. It is a Catch 22 situation!

If you are Welsh, some other special provisions apply.

The Public Records Act does not help us to proactively manage our personal information.

**Computer Misuse Act (1990)**

The act says that it is an offence to use a computer to gain unauthorised access to data and programs in any other computer.

---

Unauthorised access to computer material.

(1)A person is guilty of an offence if—

(a)he causes a computer to perform any function with intent to secure access to any program or data held in any computer, or to enable any such access to be secured ;

(b)the access he intends to secure, or to enable to be secured, is unauthorised; and

(c)he knows at the time when he causes the computer to perform the function that that is the case.

Source:http://www.legislation.gov.uk/ukpga/1990/18/crossheading /computer-misuse-offences

---

**Figure 25 - Computer Misuse Act (1990)**

The legislation ignores geographical boundaries. An offence exists whether it happens inside or outside UK jurisdiction.

Essentially, it protects us from hackers who might want to acquire our personal information.

The computer misuse act does not attempt to address the impact upon individuals whose personal data has been affected, nor does it address any possible negligence of the organisation whose systems have been hacked.

This is really about protecting the organisations that hold our personal information from possible theft of their information assets. It reinforces the consensus that organisations are the owners of your personal information.

It does not address the cause of your potential problem; there is no limit to the volume and type of personal information that is stored.

**Official Secrets Acts (1911, 1920, 1989)**

This act says that it is an offence to disclose official information in six specified categories, and where the disclosure is damaging to the national interest.

Official information is any information, document or article that a Crown Servant[41] or a government contractor has had in their possession by virtue of their position.

The categories of information are:

- Security and intelligence.
- Defence.
- International relations.
- Foreign confidences.
- Information that might lead to the commission of crime.
- The special investigation powers under the Interception of Communications Act 1985 and the Security Service Act 1989.

These are broad categories and will doubtless cover personal information.

The Act does not make any provision for us to discover whether official secrets include information about us and the Freedom of Information Act cannot help us access these records either.

---

[41]Defined as: government ministers, civil servants, including members of the diplomatic service, members of the armed forces and the police. However, the act extends to any person in possession of information from one of the categories, irrespective of how it came into their possession.

I think that we can take reassurance that Official Secrets are held in more secure government systems and are therefore less likely to be leaked or hacked.

The Act does not give us any rights to comment about, or correct the information held about us in the official secret categories. Therefore, the main issue here is really about errors and omissions. If they exist, there is not much we can do about it.

**Human Rights Act (1998)**

The Act says that it is unlawful for a public authority to act in a way that is incompatible with the European Convention on Human Rights.

Article 8 of the convention is a relevant section for our Digital Personality. This says:

> Everyone has the right to respect for his private and family life, his home and his correspondence. [42]

This may indicate that we have the right to influence the information that organisations hold about us. As personal information gradually becomes an intrinsic part of our everyday existence, I can predict that this set of legislation might become more relevant.

---

[42] Specifically Articles 2 to 12 and 14 of the Convention, Articles 1 to 3 of the First Protocol, and Article 1 of the Thirteenth Protocol – www.legislation.gov.uk/ukpga/1998/42/crossheading/introduction

Unfortunately, the Human Rights Act is drafted in such a way that it does not give you any clues as to how you might proactively exercise your rights when you want to manage the personal information held by organisations.

## Conclusion

This brief review of the most important legislation highlights a number of important points.

It confirms that the ownership of personal information is not yet been considered by UK Law to be a significant issue. The consensus is that personal information is owned by the organisation that holds it. Information can be traded, stolen, lost and leaked, and in this sense is seen simply as a commodity.

This consensus is reflected in the 2009 Department for Culture, Media and Sport and Department for Business, Innovation and Skills report entitled Digital Britain. It starts by declaring:

---

"The Digital World is a reality in all of our lives. In this report we underscore the importance of understanding, appreciating and planning for this reality"

Source– See Appendix 5

---

**Figure 26 - Digital Britain Report 2009**

The report avoids any discussion of a change in ownership rights towards personal information. Either the question has been overlooked or it has been assumed that the current consensus on ownership rights cannot change. i.e. The majority of current legislation is drafted to protect the ownership rights of the information holder not the person who is the subject of the information.

Curiously, many of our laws have provisions and clauses that recognise that errors and omissions in databases can seriously affect the daily lives of the individuals involved. In some cases, there are strong remedies and potential penalties for organisations who are cavalier about this aspect of data handling.

Legislation also seems to recognise that human beings are fallible and mendacious. Much of the law is drafted in a way that expects databases to be lost or stolen by users or criminals. This is useful if we want to punish people after an event occurs, but it does not address the real cause of our problem nor the impact it will have upon us as individuals.

As an information manager I have become aware of the legislation outlined here as part of my professional life. I am not a lawyer, however my experience tells me that UK legislation currently addresses the consequence, not the cause of information issues that concern us in our daily lives. Quite simply, with the amount of personal information held by organisations, it is inevitable that the humans who work in them will make mistakes or errors of judgement. It is a case of when, not if, it will happen.

An effective way to address this is to manage the supply of information, and to some extent legislation and UK Government's best practice is beginning to realise that this might be a way forward. However, it is early days for this sort of thinking.

I am not saying that the current law is wrong, but it is falling short of where it could be and where we need it to be. It seems that the speed of information growth has outstripped our legislators' ability to understand the emerging issues.

Our real and long-term cause for concern comes from errors and omissions in databases, not theft or fraud. The solution is better management of the data. The appropriate agent to manage the accuracy and relevance of personal information is you.

Perhaps it is now time to consider whether the ownership of personal information should be considered a "joint ownership" arrangement between the organisations and the individuals involved. This would immediately recognise the growing importance of personal information, engage people at a new level and rebalance the power from large organisations towards the individual.

If there were a legal obligation to allow people to review and amend personal information, or even to demand its deletion in some circumstances, then we would begin to see a very different approach to its use. Organisations would have to be more careful to use information in a way that was not damaging or annoying to the people involved. The penalty for not doing so would be their withdrawal of permission to use the information at all.

There would be further positive spin offs from a law that changed the ownership of personal information in this way. For example:

- The emergence of systems, devices and processes that would enable more robust ways to identify users. This would be very useful in a world where identity theft is an issue, but where most of us do not yet see the value in systems to protect our identities.

- We may see the introduction of default delete dates for personal information when it has exceeded a useful lifespan. One of the most common causes of error is the use of out of date information. Errors are exacerbated by the ability of digital technology to store everything including all of the out of date material.

- Ownership change will raise awareness of information security for all internet users. How many users still use the word "password" for their password?

- Perhaps it could also create a marketplace where organisations could trade rights over personal information with the individual owners. This could open up a massive world of micro transactions and new services.

Renegotiating personal information ownership could become vital. In a future world where our first impression of one another is delivered through social profiling techniques, errors and omissions in personal information could become career-limiting, opportunity stifling, socially obstructive and possibly irreversible.

The current law gives us remedies that we can use after errors and omissions have affected our online reputations. Once we are at this stage, it may be too late to recover.

I believe that we will eventually need different laws to help us proactively manage our own Digital Personalities.

Blank Page

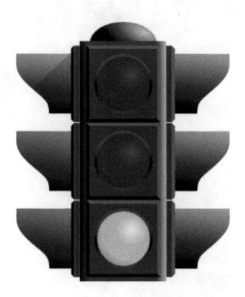

**What next?**

# Conclusion

Your Digital Personality is here to stay. It is now an unavoidable fact.

Businesses use it to determine what, when and where to sell to you. Social Profiling and Social Graphing are the tools of their trade.

Your friends and associates contribute to your Digital Personality through what they do and how they transact with you online.

You contribute to your own Digital Personality each time you transact electronically. Banking, shopping, credit cards, mortgages, telephones, internet browsing, social networking and travelling are some of the easiest ways to build up a pool of personal information.

The world is increasingly using this information to decide whether to deal with you or not.

The search result that others first see is their first impression of you and first impressions do count.

Your reactions to the growth in personal information can be either reactive or proactive

## The reactive state

You tend to be concerned primarily with privacy. You fear losing it so you want to remove information from the mix. You know that there are ways to do this and you are aware of the laws that protect us when something goes wrong.

You also know that you have to be vigilant, because our Digital Personalities are constantly building, ebbing and flowing in a digital soup that is being created for us by the many digital transactions that we conduct each day. You may be asking, "How will I keep up with all this stuff?"

## The proactive state

You recognise that a Digital Personality can be an advantage. You also recognise that a non-existent or shallow Digital Personality is sub-optimal. In some ways, this is worse than a negative image. If others cannot see anything about you, they may suspect that you have something to hide.

A negative image is also not a good result. Allowing yourself or others to publish negative or contradictory comments and information will do you no favours. You want to create and manage a good image for yourself.

A positive Digital Personality includes consistency of look and feel, a positive personality, visible and managed images and an open attitude to others of like mind. This will encourage others to interact with you.

The advantages of a well-managed Digital Personality are all about interactions. Humans love to converse and a well managed Digital Personality encourages conversation. It breaks down suspicions, builds trust and reduces risk; this encourages others to make and maintain contact with you.

Therefore, if being connected and having conversations is what a well-managed Digital Personality is all about, then it must be a good thing.

I believe that it is, but unfortunately, I am ending upon a slightly negative note.

**A warning**

There have always been people in the world who make a life out of exploiting others in a variety of ways. These people are no more or less prevalent in the digital world.

You need to protect yourself from them and understanding the ideas behind your well-managed Digital Personality can help you to do this.

Those that will try to deceive you will often have obscure or invisible Digital Personalities. You can check them out. You can even try to build a Social Graph for them. You do not have to take new people at face value.

Information about others' Digital Personalities is freely available and it can help us all to become our own digital detectives, using the available tools to protect ourselves from potential fraudsters and ID thieves.

Never accept a new digital contact at face value. Fake ones will be easy to spot. The fraudsters rarely create in-depth Digital Personalities for themselves. So look at who else they are linked to, where they have contributed (blogs and comments) and assess how complete their Digital Personality is.

A one-dimensional personality, lacking credible linkages to other similar Digital Personalities, or lacking any sense of an online history, will be a person with whom you should exercise caution. Try to find a safe, perhaps non-digital way to authenticate them before you converse or transact.

Avoiding evasive, incomplete and contradictory Digital Personalities is a good policy to follow for you to stay safe.

Active understanding and management of your Digital Personality is the best defence against those that would exploit you, because by understanding how to create a positive, helpful, open, collaborative and mutually beneficial Digital Personality, you are armed with the knowledge to help recognise the fraudulent ones.

# Appendices

## 1. PayPal's market leading T&C's

The Privacy Policy has been amended to allow PayPal to disclose certain PayPal customer information to additional third parties for the purposes set out in the table below.

**Customer Service Outsourcing**

**Who:** Convergys Customer Management Group Inc. (UK)
**Why:** To allow telephone and e-mail customer support services
**What:** Name, address, telephone number, email addresses, truncated and limited or full funding source information (case dependent), funding source expiration dates, type of PayPal account, proof of identity, account balance and transaction information, customer statements and reports, account correspondence, shipping information, promotional information.

**Credit Reference and Fraud Agencies**

**Who:** Equifax Plc (UK), CRIBIS D&B S.r.l. (Italy).
**Why:** To verify identity, make decisions concerning a customer's credit worthiness, carry out checks for the prevention and detection of crime including fraud and/or money laundering, assist in debt recovery, manage PayPal accounts and undertake statistical analysis, undertake research as to appropriateness of new products and services and system checking. Data disclosed may be retained by the applicable credit reference and fraud agency for audit and fraud prevention purposes.
**What:** Name, address, date of birth, time at address, telephone number, proof of identity, legal form, time in business, company registration number, VAT number, relevant transaction information (if appropriate).

**Who:** Bürgel Wirtschaftsinformationen GmbH & Co. KG (Germany)
**Why:** To verify identity
**What:** All account information

**Financial Products**

**Who:** PrePay Technologies Limited (trading as PrePay Solutions) (UK)
**Why:** To conduct joint marketing campaigns for PayPal pre-paid card, risk and fraud modelling, enforce terms and conditions for PayPal prepaid card
**What:** Name, address, e-mail, date of birth and account information

**Commercial Partnerships**

**Who:** Trustwave (US)
**Why:** To provide customised services and assistance to Merchants using PayPal, to facilitate the process of becoming PCI DSS compliant.
**What:** Name, e-mail address and PayPal account number

**Marketing and public relations**

**Who:** Northstar Research Partners (USA)
**Why:** To conduct customer service surveys
**What:** Name, e-mail address, type of account, type and nature of PayPal services offered or used and relevant transaction information.

**Who:** Text 100 AB (Sweden)
**Why:** To answer media enquiries regarding customer queries
**What:** Name, address, all customer account information relevant to customer queries

**Who:** Satmetrix Systems, Inc. (USA)
**Why:** To conduct customer service surveys
**What:** Name, e-mail address, type of account, type and nature of PayPal services offered or used and relevant transaction information.

**Who:** Acxiom France (France)
**Why:** To collect additional user information and better target marketing campaigns
**What:** Name, e-mail, address and phone number.

**Who:** Adelanto (France)
**Why:** To execute marketing campaigns for merchants
**What:** Name of the merchant, name of the contact person, e-mail, address, merchant website URL, type and nature of PayPal services offered or used.

**Who:** Consultix (France and Spain) and Quadro Srl (Italy)

**Why:** To host information provided by merchants and display part of this information on the pages of the PayPal website listing websites accepting PayPal and proposing special offers to PayPal users.

**What:** All information provided by merchants in connection with their use of these pages of the PayPal website (including in particular name of the merchant, name of the contact, email, logo and information relating to the promotion(s) offered to PayPal users).

**Operational services**

**Who:** Blue Media S.A. (Poland)
**Why:** To verify identity and ensure that a user is a PayPal account holder. To process instant funding requests made by a user through the Blue Media services.
**What:** Name, e-mail address.

**Who:** Consultix GmbH (Germany)
**Why:** To assist in the creation of PayPal Business Accounts for merchants on-boarding through their bank's payment gateway
**What:** All information provided by the merchant (directly or via his bank) for the purpose of creating his PayPal business account (including without limitation email address, address, business name, business contact details and bank account details)

## 2. Standard communication requesting information deletion

Your name
Your address
Postcode
Phone number
Your email(s)

Date

The Data Manager
X Ltd
X's address

Dear Sir/Madam,

PERSONAL INFORMATION DELETION REQUEST

Please could you EITHER DELETE OR make ANONYMOUS all information that you hold on me and CONFIRM to me what action you have taken to ensure my information is not re-introduced to any of your databases.

I understand that I do not have an automatic entitlement to this request, but I am asking you because I believe there is no valid business or other reason for you to hold information about me.

I am a private person and I am making this request because you can help me to limit the spread of my personal information.

Yours truly,

Sign here

Your Name

## 3. Standard communication for a Subject Access Request

Your name
Your address
Postcode
Phone number
Your email(s)

Date

The Data Manager
X Ltd
X's address
X's postcode

Dear Sir/Madam,

SUBJECT ACCESS REQUEST

Please could you send me all information that you hold on me that I am entitled to under section 7(1) of the Data Protection Act 1998?

Yours truly,

Sign here

Your Name

## 4. Standard communication to opt out of the Edited Electoral Roll

Your name
Your address
Postcode
Phone number

Date

The Electoral Registration Office
Local Authority address

Dear Sir / Madam,

I wish to opt out of the Edited Version of the electoral register.

MY NAME:

MY ADDRESS:

Please confirm when this has been request has been completed.

Yours truly,

Sign here


Your Name

## 5. Digital Britain Report June 2009

On 26 August 1768, when Captain James Cook set sail for Australia, it took 2 years and 320 days before he returned to describe what he found there.
Yesterday, on 15 June 2009, 20 hours of new content were posted on YouTube every minute, 494 exabytes of information were transferred seamlessly across the globe, over 2.6 billion mobile minutes were exchanged across Europe, and millions of enquiries were made using a Google algorithm.
The Digital World is a reality in all of our lives. In this report we underscore the importance of understanding, appreciating and planning for this reality and we seek to achieve the following:
1.      An analysis of the levels of digital participation, skills and access needed for the digital future, with a plan for increasing participation, and more coherent public structures to deal with it.
2.      An analysis of our communications infrastructure capabilities, an identification of the gaps and recommendations on how to fill them.
3.      A statement of ambition for the future growth of our creative industries, proposals for a legal and regulatory framework for intellectual property in a digital world, proposals on skills and a recognition of the need for investment support and innovation.
4.      A restatement of the need for specific market intervention in the UK content market, and what that will demand of the BBC and its role in Digital Britain. What that means for the future of the C4 Corporation. An analysis of the importance of other forms of independent and suitably funded news, and what clarification and changes are needed to the existing framework.
5.      An analysis of the skills, research and training markets, and what supply side issues need addressing for a fully functioning digital economy.
6.      A framework for digital security and digital safety at international and national levels and recognition that in a world of high speed connectivity we need a digital framework not an analogue one.
7.      A review of what all of this means for the Government and how digital governance in the information age demands new structures, new safeguards, and new data management, access and transparency rules.

Source: Department for Culture, Media and Sport and Department for Business, Innovation and Skills - Digital Britain Final Report - Crown Copyright - ISBN: 9780101765022

## 6. Table of Figures